ERNEST HEMINGWAY

The Iceberg Theory

THE HISTORY HOUR

CONTENTS

INTRODUCTION

❦

Ernest Miller Hemingway is one of the most interesting characters you will ever read about in your life.

❦

After reaching the age of being able to join the war effort his journeys in life only had begun. He traveled everywhere with excuses to write. While on his adventures he would meet new women who interested him and flirt with them unbounded even in front of his wives; most of who seemed to be used to all of it.

❦

He loved big game hunting and large fishing expeditions and

to brag about his many catches and hunts. His bragging was so big that everyone knew he had to be lying.

***

He predicted at a young age that he would commit suicide like his father. Suicide ran rampant in the Hemingway family. You will find in the book why the Hemingways all committed suicide.

***

When it came to his collection of six-toed cats, he was a bowl of jelly. He melted like butter and spoke softly and cuddled them like they were all royalty. His cats never had to want for anything. He had an extreme attachment to all of his pets.

***

Ernest's life did not go out large as he lived. It was quiet, in an area where no one would find his burial grounds for quite some time and for years the public had no idea that he had committed suicide.

***

Killing himself at 61 seemed to have cut a brilliant man's life very short when he was beginning to become famous worldwide.

***

Read on to see what you think.

❧ II ❧
ERNEST BIRTH AND
YOUNGER YEARS

«The world breaks everyone, and afterward, some are
strong at the broken places.»

Ernest Hemingway

❦

Ernest Hemingway was the first son born to Grace Hall and
Clarence Edmonds Hemingway in the suburbs of Chicago,
Illinois. The newborn was named after his mother's grandfa-
ther, Ernest Hall and his mom's uncle, Miller Hall. Clarence
Hemingway was a country doctor who took the time to teach
Ernest the sports of hunting and fishing.

❦

His mother, Grace, being a religious woman, was active in
their church. She had Ernest busy playing the cello and

singing in the church choir. Hemingway had a hard time in his early years fighting off his mother's feminine influences while at the same time pulling on the forces of his father the physician.

۞

When he was but a child, Ernest's mom would dress him up like a girl and put him in flowery hats that had ribbons on them and lacy white dresses. She made sure his hair stayed long. He called his mom "*Fweetee*" for Sweetie, and she always called him her "*Dutch Doll*y." Ernest got tired of it all. He would tell her,

"I am not a Dutch doll, Bang! I shoot Fweetee."

Years later he would find himself being beaten by his Dad using a razor strap, so Ernest would hide somewhere with a loaded shotgun and place his dad's head within the crosshairs.

۞

Ernest having been educated in public schools started his writing in high school, where he had developed an outstanding personality and active in writing projects. Ernest played all kinds of sports and served as the track team manager, and he excelled in all his grades. He had a tremendous talent for writing and wrote for the school's yearbook called the Tabula, and the school's newspaper called the Trapeze; usually humorous articles. It was in the Oak Park School System that Ernest was able to see the first of his writings become published, while at times he used the pen name of Ring Lardner, Jr.

Spending his summers with his family on Walloon Lake in the northern woods of Michigan where he would go on doctor calls with his dad were what mattered the most to him. They always stayed in the family's summer house, Windemere.

Ernest kept himself busy exploring the land, squirrel hunting, other small game, and fishing all the streams that fed into Lake Michigan. The fishing and hunting would remain two of Ernest's favorite hobbies throughout his entire life, but he always preferred to go after the big game and the big fish.

It seems odd that even with the intense pleasure that Ernest with all his popularity in high school and the outdoor life he enjoyed so much – that he was able to show himself as a distinguished athlete and scholar – he still ran away from his secure home life two times.

When Ernest graduated from High School in 1917, he decided to not go to college as his parents thought he would. Instead, he became a "*cub*" reporter working for the Kansas City Star newspaper. The job had been arranged by his Uncle Tyler who at the time was close friends with the chief editorial writer for the paper.

ERNEST, WWI AND PAULINE PFEIFFER

«The best way to find out if you can trust somebody is to trust them.»

Ernest Hemingway

❧

Ernest wanted badly to join the war effort in World War I but he was rejected over and over for any military service because he had a bad eye, but he finally was able to enter for an ambulance driver position for the American Red Cross.

❧

July 8, 1918, and Ernest had not turned nineteen years old he was injured at the Austro-Italian front. He had first gone to Paris after reaching Europe, traveled on to Milan after getting his orders in the first part of June. The very day he got there, an ammunition factory exploded, and Ernest found himself carrying more mutilated bodies and unfortunately body parts to a morgue that had been thrown together just for this purpose; this was a terrible way to be initiated to all the horrors of war.

Ernest was decorated for his heroism and placed in a hospital in Milan where he fell madly in love with a Red Cross nurse, one Agnes von Kurowsky and she would not marry him. It would become some of his experiences that he would never forget.

Ernest decided to enlist in the medical division of the Red Cross by driving an ambulance at the Italian front. He became severely wounded in his knee, but still carried a man who had been injured on his back a far distance to get him to an aid station and while on the way there Ernest was hit in his legs by several bullets from a machine gun.

Ernest had over two hundred bullet fragments taken from his legs and his body. After healing from the wounds, he then enlisted in the infantry for Italy, served on the front lines of Austria until the truce, then decorated for his bravery by the government of Italy. Ernest returned home soon after where he was also called a hero.

Italy said he gave generous assistance to Italian soldiers who were more seriously hurt by that same explosion but would not allow anyone to help him until everyone else was evacuated.

❧

Ernest described the scene and one of the most terrible noises you will sometimes hear on the front. He said he died then. He felt his soul or whatever it was coming out, leaving his body, just like you would pull a handkerchief out from your pocket. He went on to say that his soul flew all around him and came back into his body again and he was no longer dead. It sounds like one of the many near-death experiences we read about so many times today.

❧

When Ernest came home from Italy at the beginning of 1919, he felt that Oak Park was dull after the excitement of war, seeing the beauty he had in foreign lands and having had the romance of one woman older than he, Agnes von Kurowsky.

❧

At this time he was only nineteen years old and had only been out of high school for eighteen months, but the war itself and matured him far beyond his years.

❧

Living with his Mom and Dad, who had never seemed to appreciate what Ernest had lived through in the war, was hard for him. He had not been home long when they started pressuring him to either further his education or compel him to get a job, but at this point in his life, Ernest could not seem to get interested in much of anything. One would probably say with the medical knowledge we have now that he was probably suffering from depression, PTSD or worse.

⚜

Ernest moved to Chicago in 1920 in the fall and started writing for the Star Weekly. He was living with a friend when he met Hadley Richardson, and the two fell quickly in love. Hadley and Ernest got married September 1921, and in November Ernest was offered a job to start working for the Toronto Daily Star for its European Correspondent.

⚜

Earnest and Hadley would be leaving for Paris, France where all of the literature had been changing by writers like James Joyce, Ezra Pound, Ford Maddox Ford, and Gertrude Stein. Ernest was not going to miss out on his chance to change it as well.

⚜

The new Hemingways made it to Paris December 22, 1921, and within a few weeks, they had moved into what would be their first apartment together at 74 rue Cardinal Lemoine. It turned out to be a miserable place to live as it had a bathroom which was nothing but a closet that contained a slop bucket and no running water.

⚜

Ernest did try to minimize the primitiveness of their living quarters for his wife who had been one that was brought up in a high lifestyle. Despite the rough living conditions, Hadley endured as she carried along with Ernest's enthusiasm in living his bohemian lifestyle. It is said to have been despite the lack of money, their poor living conditions, that these were as told by Ernest the happiest years of his life and the most productive artistically.

❧

But the ironic part is they had the money to live in a lovely apartment; with Hadley's trust fund and the job, Hemingway had procured it made their annual income total $3,000 which was a decent sum even in the inflated economies in Europe during that time. Ernest then rented a room at 39 rue Descartes so he could write in peace. One is not sure of the condition of that room.

❧

Due to having a letter of introduction from one Sherwood Anderson, Ernest was able to meet some of the prominent artists and writers of Paris and was able to forge some quick friendships with those famous people during those first few years he was living in Paris.

❧

Among those considered friends were Gertrude Stein, James Joyce, Lincoln Steffens, Wyndham Lewis, Ezra Pound, Sylvia Beach, Max Eastman and was also acquainted with a couple of famous painters by the names of Picasso and Miro. The friendships would prove to be instrumental in Ernest's career as an artist and a writer.

⁂

Ernest had just started making a name as a reporter as well as a fledgling fiction writer, and right as Ernest and Hadley were making their stride in the social society of Europe, they realized that they were going to have a baby; it would be their first child. They wanted their new baby to be born in North America where they felt the hospitals and physicians were much better. So the Hemingways left Paris in 1923 and moved to Toronto, and Ernest began writing for the Toronto Daily Star as they waited for their first baby to arrive.

⁂

October 10th, 1923, John Hadley Nicanor Hemingway was born, and in January of 1924, the Hemingway family boarded their ship as they went back to Paris where Ernest would work to finish making his name known.

⁂

Also during 1923, Ernest turned out his first book that was published, "***Three Stories and Ten Poems***." The poems seem insignificant, but the stories contained therein give one a strong indication of Ernest's real emerging genius.

⁂

In 1925 with his book "***In Our Time***" Ernest pulled from his experiences when he had summered on Lake Michigan to show the initiation into a world of violence and pain of a young Nick Adams, who would later serve as a model for Hemingway's heroes.

৩৫৩

1926 came, and Ernest published the novel, "***The Sun Also Rises***," which he considered to be his first real success. It was pessimistic and at the same time, a sparkling book, and dealt with an entire group of expatriates who were aimless in Spain and France - who were members in the postwar "***Lost Generation***," a phrase used by Hemingway that he scorned while at the same time he made it famous. In this work, it put him in the limelight, and he had carved it out while at the same time resented it for the last part of his life. His book "***The Torrents of Spring***," which was a parody of American author Sherwood Anderson's published book "***Dark Laughter***," that had also been published in 1926.

৩৫৩

Book writing seemed to occupy Ernest for most of his postwar years. He stayed in Paris for his base, but he continued to travel a lot so as not to miss out on bullfighting, skiing, hunting and fishing and a lot of it had made the background for most of his writing.

৩৫৩

Ernest's mastery of short fiction was advanced by the book "***Men Without Women***" in 1927 and became thoroughly established along with the stories in the book of "***Winner Take Nothing***" in 1933. Among some of his finest stories are

"The Killers," "*The Short Happy Life of Francis Macomber*," and "*The Snows of Kilimanjaro*."

❧

As far as the public cared, his novel "*A Farewell to Arms*" in 1929 would overshadow all those works. In reaching back to his time as a young soldier while in Italy, Ernest completed what turned out to be a grim but a tremendously powerful, lyrical novel that weaved a war story with a love story.

❧

In the book, while he was serving in the Italian ambulance service all during World War I, Frederic Henry, the American lieutenant falls in love with his English nurse by the name of Catherine Barkley, who takes care of him during his recovery after having been wounded. Catherine gets pregnant by Frederic, but he has to get back to his post.

❧

Frederic deserts the army during the disastrous retreat of the Italians after the great Battle of Caporetto, and the young reunited couple run from Italy by escaping across the border into the wilds of Switzerland. Catherine and the baby die while she is giving birth; Henry is devastated with losing the greatest love of his life.

❧

It seemed he could not do any wrong in his writing career, but in his personal life, it appeared it had started to show signs of wear. So, Ernest divorced his first wife, Hadley in 1927 after only six years of marriage.

※

Later that same year in 1927, Ernest married one Pauline Pfeiffer, who was a fashion reporter who occasionally wrote for Vogue and Vanity Fair. Ernest and Pauline left for Key West, Florida from Paris in 1928 to search for some new surroundings for the new life they had started together. They lived there for almost twelve years. Ernest loved it there for playing and working, and he discovered the world of big game fishing.

※

Ernest converted (not sure what the process was in 1927) to Catholicism to marry one Pauline Pfeiffer. In 1928, Ernest moved to Florida to the Key West, Florida area.

※

It was in 1928, when Ernest's father, Dr. Clarence Hemingway stayed at his medical office practice for the entire morning, then went home for lunch. He methodically burned some of his papers downstairs in his basement furnace. He then walked up their stairs to where his bedroom was on the second floor, and the room lay in the semi-darkness because the shades were pulled, he sat on the edge of their marital bed.

※

In the room next to where he was sitting, Leicester, his 13-year son, had a cold and was laying down in his bed when he heard a gunshot in his father's bedroom. He ran and knocked on his Dad's bedroom door and hollered out for his Father. When Leicester went inside, it was darker in the bedroom because of the drawn shades, there lay his dad on the bed, but breathing hoarsely Leicester went and placed his hand behind his Dad's head; he could feel the sticky, warm blood on his hand.

❦

Dr. Charles had become very ill with heart disease, diabetes and some physical ailments that seemed to be exacerbating what was already a weak mental state; he had been suffering from some losses over some bad investments that he had made in some real estate deals in Florida and was depressed. Dr. Charles took his father's .32 revolver made by Smith & Wesson, pressed the barrel behind his right ear and shot himself.

❦

At the time Ernest was in Trenton, New Jersey as he was traveling back to his home in Key West, he received a telegram with the news of his father's suicide.

❦

Still, in shock, he went immediately to Oak Park to take care of the financial arrangements and the funeral. Afterward, he went back home; as he was determined not to let his Father's suicide keep him from finally finishing "*A Farewell to Arms*."

❦

Ernest told his editor, Max Perkins, that he was fond of his father, and he felt terrible about all that had happened. But, he felt he had to throw himself into his work and try to put this behind him so he could finish his book like he had wanted so he would be able to support his family financially. He guessed the part that he felt so sad about was that it was his father is who he had cared about the most.

❦

Dr. Clarence's death would still haunt Ernest for the rest of his life. The family, seemingly embarrassed by the fact of suicide, stayed with the story that financial and health issues were reasons for his death, the real unspoken worry among them was that insanity being the culprit and being such a stigma would get out to the public.

❦

Ernest would not talk about this possibility but still admitted soon after the suicide that he, Ernest, would probably die the same way. Ernest decided to blame others for his father's death: first being he wanted to blame his uncle because he gave his dad some bad investment advice, and then he refused to help him with a loan, then he accused his mother, Grace, his hatred would keep growing like a festered boil till he could stand it no longer.

❦

Ernest admitted that he hated his mother when he realized all that she was and all the things she had done to '*him*' as a child and the way she had treated his dad. He also said he loved his dad, but he still embarrassed me terribly by his cowardice. He felt that his mom was the all American bitch, and she would be able to make a pack mule shoot himself: and for sure his poor father.

***

As time marched on, Ernest would become callous about both of his parents. He had divulged to one of his friends that if he had known his dad was contemplating suicide, he would have paid him off to postpone the suicide until after he completed his book.

***

Ernest once said that his Dad's suicide was the best story that he had *never* written about; in one of his books, he had written that his dad was a coward and had killed himself for no reason. However, he took that statement out before the book was published.

***

Ernest kept a strong desire to make his father look like a coward, and it seemed to become a strong theme in his writing. He even portrayed what he felt was his Dad's weakness in character in his books "**The Doctor and the Doctor's Wife**" and "**Fathers and Sons**."

***

The new Hemingways had heard about Key West from one of

Ernest's friends by the name of John Dos Passos, so Ernest and Pauline had stopped at this tiny Florida delight on their way back to the states from Paris. They soon found out that life contained in Key West was a lot like them living in some foreign country but still sitting perched on the very southern tip of the United States.

Ernest fell in love with it. He said it was the best place he had ever been anywhere, at any time, tamarind trees, flowers, coconut palms, and guava trees. They rented an apartment, then a house for about two years and then they bought a large house located at 907 Whitehead Street by the help of $12,500 from Uncle Gus, Pauline's wealthy relative.

At the time, Pauline was pregnant and on June 28th, 1928 she gave birth to Patrick by cesarean section. Two years later in 1931, Gregory was born, their second son, and the last of Ernest's children.

There were so many places that Hemingway would write and so many that most people do not even know about. One such gem was in Piggott, Arkansas that appears only as a blip of a dot on a map when you first look at it. If you take a closer look, you will notice that Piggott lies in Northeast Arkansas, near the bootheel of Missouri.

It was here that Ernest wrote part of "**A Farewell to Arms**" and several short stories while he would be visiting in Piggott. I am sure you must be speculating as to how in the world did he find this little hole in the wall of a town named Piggott. I would ask you the same question if I did not know the answer.

❧

While Ernest and Pauline were in Paris, France and still married, they would also spend time with her family in Piggott, Arkansas, it all took place in the late 1920s and the 1930s when Ernest was still struggling as a writer.

❧

His in-laws, the Pfeiffers were the apparent part of the entire equation and attractive to others by their right. They were some of the key leaders in Clay County where Piggott was founded. They held more than 60,000 acres in land holdings.

❧

Pauline's father would drain and then convert the swamp lands to 40 or 80-acre tracts for tenant farmers. He was known as a compassionate, generous man. It was during the Great Depression when people of Piggott fell on tough times; he would give odd jobs to anybody who would ask, most of the time by letting people paint his house even if it did not need painting.

❧

Ernest was full of drama and could sure show his flair for this quality. He once wrote to his x-mother-in-law, Mrs. Pfeiffer in Piggott, Arkansas in 1936 about how hard he had been working. About how he had gone through a spell where he had felt pretty gloomy and not slept for almost three weeks. Ernest went on to tell her that he would get up about two in the morning and write until daylight.

❧

It seemed when you were writing a book that your brain will race all the time until you get up and write all the stuff inside your head so by the next morning you feel exhausted. The explanation of this mood and some of the other mood episodes he talked about, suggests that Ernest probably suffered during his adult life from Bipolar Disorder and this description was part of one of his manic phases, but he also seemed to suffer from along with other comorbid mental problems.

❧

It was in 1937 that he went abroad to Spain as a reporter to narrate on Spains Civil War, his basis "***For Whom the Bell Tolls***." Ernest and Pauline were separated by supporting the opposing sides on this Civil War, and his response to this was to leave the Catholic church.

❧

After Ernest's x-mother-in-law, Mary Pfeiffer died, the home place was sold with all furnishings to the family of Tom Janes in 1950. They worked at preserving the house, contents, and grounds for years and finally sold it all to Arkansas State University in 1997. You will find the property listed in the

National Historic Register as well as Arkansas State University's Heritage Sites list, which is the properties of national and regional significance for the Arkansas Delta.

If you ever get to visit this fantastic place, Hemingway-Pfeiffer Home in Piggott, Ark., you will see three buildings you can tour. Because of those who have taken such precious care; today it still contains 75% of its original furniture.

You will be able to see Pauline and Ernest's bedroom like it was in 1930. The kitchen is truly authentic as it has the original farmhouse sink.

When the property was getting a facelift, the Pfeiffer house was noted for having over fifty layers of the exterior paint. That would decipher to fifty odd jobs for someone needing work during the depression.

The studio out in the barn where Ernest would write is now filled with photos and information on the safari adventures that Pauline and Ernest took with a detailed timeline of the life of Ernest while with the Pfeiffers.

The Karl and Matilda Pfeiffer's house holds a fantastic gem and mineral collection you will not want to miss.

The grounds around the house and barn place look almost the same as they once did during the 1930s with its heirloom flowers, the towering trees, and an old clothesline in the backyard.

❧ IV ❧
STORIES OF WAR

«All things truly wicked start from innocence.»

Ernest Hemingway

❦

Ernest had a genuine love for Spain and for some reason a strong passion for bullfighting that served as his base for **"*Death in the Afternoon*,"** with bullfighting he saw as a spectators sport because he felt it was more of a tragic type of ceremony instead of an actual competition.

❦

As was the case with a safari he participated in during 1933-34 in the region of Tanganyika where the **"*big-game*"** resided. The safari resulted in the book of **"*Green Hills of Africa*"** (1935), with an accounting of what else but big-game hunting.

He purchased a home in Key West, Florida just because he loved fishing so much and even bought a fishing boat. There he wrote what others called a 'minor' novel in 1937 called "**To Have and Have Not**" that was about a desperado in the Caribbean set in a background where there was upper-class decadence and lower-class violence in Key West at the time of the Great Depression.

By now, Spain found itself in the middle of a civil war. Hemingway found himself attached to Spain and made at least four different trips there, finding himself a correspondent once again. He worked at raising money for the group of Republicans for their struggles against the Nationalist party under General Franco. From these experiences, he wrote a play he named "The Fifth Column" (1938), which he set the background in the besieged country of Madrid.

As he wrote in most of his books, the hero in the play was always based on the author. After he made his last visit to the Spanish War, he bought Finca Vigia (Lookout Farm), an estate that was surely not pretentious that lay outside Havana, Cuba and from there he left to work as a war correspondent to cover another war – when the Japanese invaded China.

Ernest again took another job, when he decided to cover the Chinese-Japanese war during 1941. He was traveling with

Martha, his wife and would write dispatches about what was going on with the fight for PM magazine. It turned out to a very tedious trip, and Ernest was ever so glad to get back to Cuba for some rest. He was tired. But, he did not stay long.

❧

The stories Ernest gathered in Spain during wartime and peacetime became the novel «*For Whom the Bell Tolls*» (1940), that became an impressive and substantial work that some of the critics would consider his best novel, over his book "*A Farewell to Arms*." It was the most successful of any his books when measured by the number of sales.

❧

Being set at the time of the Spanish Civil War, the book tells of Robert Jordan, who is an American Volunteer that had been sent there to join a guerrilla group behind the Nationalist lines located in the Guadarrama Mountains.

❧

The central part of the novel deals with the main character and how he related with the rest of the personalities of those in the band, inclusive of the girl Maria, the one with who he fell in love. Through flashbacks, discussion, and different stories, Ernest tells the vivid profiles of the different Spanish characters and leaves no one wondering about the inhumanity and cruelty that was stirred up by the civil war.

❧

The hero's mission was to blow up a bridge that was strategic to both sides located near Segovia there to aid the Republican attack that was coming; one he knew was doomed all along to fail. He could feel it in the air like electricity jumping around him making it an impending disaster, so he blows up that very bridge but becomes wounded and has his comrades leave him there in the rubble, where he attempts to prepare for the last minute retaliation to all of the Nationalist that were pursuing him.

❦

Ernest's entire life seemed to live for the fascination of war; in *"A Farewell to Arms"* he focused on how pointless it was, in his book *"For Whom the Bell Tolls"* is about the comradeship it makes – and as World War II waged on, Ernest made his way on to London working as a journalist.

❦

Ernest traveled to Spain in March of 1937, so he could cover the Civil War of Spain for the '**North American Newspaper Alliance**.'

❦

The same civil war also caused a conflict in the marriage at the Hemingway home too. Ernest met another young writer who struck his fancy by the name of Martha Gellhorn there in Key West, and the two of them started conducting a secret affair that lasted almost four years.

❦

Pauline had been siding with the Fascist group Franco

Regime located in Spain only because of its stance towards pro-catholic, and Ernest was supporting communist loyalists who were supporting the elected democratic government.

❦

The story goes that Ernest was at a pub in Key West, Florida called '**Sloppy Joe's**' when all of a sudden he was taken by a beautiful woman with the name of Martha Gellhorn. Ernest did not lose any time introducing himself to Martha, and he even introduced her to Pauline on the same day. The situation was nerve-racking because Martha kept coming to visit Ernest at Pauline's home in Key West.

❦

There was one night, after dinner, Martha and Ernest stepped out to sit on the veranda. Ernest became affectionate and called Martha "**daughter**." It sure seemed a weird nickname for a woman who was much younger than you and that you had already shown a definite romantic attraction.

❦

Ernest filled up her glass and asked Martha if she had ever had the opportunity to "**go to a bullfight**." Martha told him she had not, so Ernest was inspired and told her,

"then we will go."

Ernest went back inside the house for a few minutes, and Martha found herself once again sitting on the veranda alone, and she felt out of place.

Ernest stepped back out on the veranda and asked Martha
and said,

"penny for your thoughts?"

Martha said to him,

"I was sitting there thinking about life, not ever
knowing what is coming next, and who you might
meet."

Ernest told her with the conviction that he knew when he
first laid eyes on her, that she was the woman he had been
waiting for and the one he had to marry.

Martha expressed her doubts about whether Ernest was even
sincere and about their brief interlude of romance. She saw a
book lying on a table and asked him about it; Ernest told her
it was

"Death in the Afternoon. I have signed it for you; it is
for you."

Martha opened up the book and saw the words,

"For the woman who I am going wed. Ernest. Key
West, 1937."

Martha was insistent that he went away with her to Spain
and told him how concerned she was about the war going on

there. Ernest told her he would work out all the details and would indeed go with her. Ernest walked her back to the hotel where she had been staying, and kissed her again as he said,

"goodnight daughter."

That night Martha was laying in bed going over what had happened that evening and what lies ahead in Spain. She knew that Ernest was sincere about wanting to marry her and when she went to sleep, she knew that she wished the same as well.

❧

It wasn't long before Ernest was able to join Martha in Spain where they began covering the civil war. During the time in Spain, Ernest's marriage to Pauline continued to deteriorate, ending in divorce November 1940.

❧

Since Ernest was always traveling with Gellhorn, they fell in love as they kept competing for quality articles. The loyalist movement failed, and the rebels led by Franco won the war and decided on a government of dictatorship in the spring of 1939. Ernest's side lost the war, but he used his experiences to write his novel "***For Whom the Bell Tolls***," and a play titled "***The Fifth Column***" along with many short stories.

❧

It was during the 1940s that Ernest was working on what would be considered the heavily edited and published posthumously novels "*Islands In The Stream*" and "*The Garden of Eden*." He would cover World War II, then divorce Martha Gellhorn, his third wife, and many say he participated in WWII and quickly married a fourth wife, Mary Welsh.

❦

November 21st, 1940 Ernest married Martha in Cheyenne, Wyoming. It would just be a short while before they would make their home in Cuba.

❦

After Ernest's popular and critical success of his book "*For Whom the Bell Tolls*," Ernest seemed to lapse into a somewhat literary silence that lasted an entire decade but appeared to be the result of his frequently reckless, strenuous, activities he encountered during WWII.

❦

By 1942 Ernest decided to take on an undercover operation and hunt down some German submarines out in the Atlantic ocean somewhere off Cuba's coast. Ernest got some of his friends together and outfitted his boat '*The Pilar*' with some extra fuel tanks, radio equipment, a good quantity of artillery with high hopes if he could find a German sub he would get in close enough so he could drop a bomb down the sub's hatch.

❦

Ernest called his gang the "*Crook Factory*." Nothing came of their expedition except for having a good time drinking and fishing, and in their process, it irritated Martha who was sure Ernest was avoiding his responsibilities as a writer to report what was going on in the real war that was raging in Europe.

❧

In 1942, Ernest would witness some of the most horrible bloody battles to be seen in Europe. At the time he was given the nickname of "**Papa**" by his admirers, both literary and military.

❧

And again, it was there, Martha and Ernest were apart for a time, Ernest again ran into another female who was a journalist by the name of Mary Welsh who lived in Minnesota.

❧

He found Mary was nothing like Martha. She has short blonde hair, tiny, and had a boyish look. She seemed to dress unflatteringly that made her look a little ordinary and more like a middle-class girl. She had been described as

'not good looking, but cute, and a good figure.'

There seemed to be something about Mary though that attracted Ernest immediately. Mary had been a woman that before meeting Ernest had enjoyed what others referred to as "*the good life*," and that had included being in the company of men, so she was already a fan of Ernest's.

❧

May 1944 rolled around, and Ernest decided he should get to Europe so he could report on the war, he went first to London so he could write about the RAF and the effects the war was having on England.

※

While he was there, Ernest was injured in a motor vehicle car crash where he suffered a severe concussion and a large gash on his head that needed 50 stitches.

※

Martha came to see him in the hospital and acted like his injuries were nothing, scolding him for getting involved in a wreck because he was drunk. Ernest was genuinely hurt, and Martha acted like this was the beginning of the end of another marriage.

※

While Ernest was in London, he met Mary Welsh, the opposite of Martha. Mary was adoring, complimentary, and caring while Martha did not care at all, she had lost any care or admiration for Ernest and often insulted him. For Ernest, it was an easy choice between the women, so he fell in love with the woman who liked him.

※

There she was, carrying in daffodils, and it seemed like it pleased Ernest a lot. Before she left his room, Ernest told her that he would be back in Dortch in a couple of days and for her to come to see him.

Ernest was flying several missions for the Royal Air Force and even crossed over the English Channel with other American troops on D-Day (June 6, 1944.) He attached himself to the 4th Infantry Division of the 22nd Regiment. Ernest saw so much action in Normandy and while in the Battle of the Bulge that it was burned in his memories. He helped participate in liberating Paris, and even though he was a journalist, he still impressed the professional soldiers not just as a man of courage during battle, but as an expert with military matters, intelligence collection, and guerrilla activities.

AFTER THE WAR – ERNEST
LIVED LIFE LARGE

❧

H e had one encounter that was extremely flirtatious. There was found an article entitled, Ernest is in love: four letters were found, they provide some of the intimate details that characterize what motives there were in Ernest's and Jigee Viertel's (wife of screenwriter, Peter Viertel) behind their relationship. Peter Viertel felt that Mary might have mistaken Ernest's seductive advances toward Jigee. Jigee was not wealthy and never would have been able to support him in the luxury he had grown accustomed.

❧

Peter Viertel was curious like Mary about Jigee's growing love with Ernest but had not realized that Mary was getting so upset about their growing love affair. Peter was getting more and more conscious when his dad started showering all the attention toward Jigee. But it confused him as to why Mary acted like she was overlooking the entire affair.

৯✹৩

Jigee told Peter when they would be by themselves, that he did not have to worry or be jealous because their devotion to each other was nothing but platonic as Ernest needed being

«a little bit of in love with someone so he could feel
more alive.»

She did admit to Peter that she loved Ernest's adoration, but said it was utterly absurd for anyone to be jealous.

৯✹৩

Ernest seemed to go through women like he went through changing underwear.

৯✹৩

First, his marriage to Hadley Richardson, the mother to son number one; two, Pauline Pfeiffer, she was the mother of sons #2 and #3; then his marriage to Martha Gellhorn with all of them ending in divorce. After the war, Ernest and wife #4, Mary bought a home near to Havana, Cuba.

৯✹৩

Ernest started writing hard again. He traveled a lot too, and while he was on a trip into Africa, he got injured in another plane crash. Ernest was awarded the Pulitzer Prize for fiction in 1953 for his book '**The Old Man and the Sea**" (1952), which was a short heroic novel written about an elderly Cuban fisherman, that after struggling for a very long time, the boats and hooks and a giant marlin are eaten by hungry sharks during the voyage home. A year later in 1953, he won the Nobel Prize for Literature.

In 1954 Ernest's physical condition was declining even more, and it seemed his mental problems were getting more severe and starting to have an impact on his literary output during the last few years of his life. Their journey into Africa that had been planned by Ernest and his wife ended with their plane crashing in the Belgian Congo.

The crash was much worse than the other as Ernest's skull was fractured, two of the discs in his spine fractured, his right shoulder and arm dislocated, his right kidney, his liver, and spleen were all ruptured, his sphincter muscle became paralyzed due to the compressed vertebrae affecting the iliac nerve.

It caused him to have no control over his bowels. His head, face, and arms had been burned badly by the planes flames, leaving his hearing and vision impaired. He suffered from diarrhea, anthrax, skin cancers, diabetes, high blood pressure, malaria, and hepatitis. One biographer noted that anyone who would have been less robust than Ernest would never have lived through all of that could have been able to commit suicide.

Ernest suffered from injuries from which he never recovered along with his severe burns. An additional strain was added when the Cuban government Revolutionary of Fidel Castro forced Ernest and his wife to leave Cuba.

❦ V ❦
ERNEST'S UNCONSUMMATED LOVE AFFAIR

«Never go on trips with anyone you do not love.»

Ernest Hemingway

❦

It seems that Ernest also developed quite a fondness for Marlene Dietrich. Their story was made clear in that their feelings for each other were mutual but never consummated.

❦

Ernest and Marlene met during 1934 while on a French luxury ocean liner, the Ile de France, while Ernest was making his journey back to Key West after a safari deep in east Africa. Dietrich was on her way back to Hollywood after she had been visiting some of her relatives living in Nazi Germany;

unknowing this would be one of her last trips home. For them, it was absolutely

"Love when they first saw each other"

on that French luxury ocean liner.

❀❀❀

The affair lasted during his marriage to Pauline Pfeiffer. He and Pauline did not divorce until 1940.

❀❀❀

Marlene Dietrich was born as Marie Magdalene Dietrich in Berlin during 1901 and had been fortunate enough to become an entertainer, actress, and singer. She had studied violin before she got a job as actress and chorus girl in Vienna and Berlin during the 1920s.

❀❀❀

Three years later in 1923, she burst into stardom. She went on to have the starring role in '***Shanghai Express***' and '***The Scarlet Empress***,' and they both cemented her status as a femme fatale. After Dietrich went on to Hollywood instead of becoming nothing but a puppet for the Nazi regime, at which time she was designated as a traitor by the Germans for decades to come. Marlene was known best for her singing; some of her most famous tunes were '***Lili Marlene***' and '***Falling in Love Again***.'

❀❀❀

There have been a set of unpublished telegrams and letters totaling 30 between Ernest Hemingway and Marlene Dietrich, which are now being made public for the first time in history. They reveal the real depth of the passion they had for each other; as hard as it is to believe they NEVER had a sexual encounter.

❦

The Kennedy Library located in Boston by the instructions of Maria Riva, Dietrich's daughter, wanted their letters to be kept private for at least fifteen years after Marlene Dietrich's death.

❦

It seems that Dietrich and Ernest began their correspondence with each other when she was 47 and he was 50 and stayed in contact until Ernest committed suicide in 1961. Again, they never consummated the love they had for each other due to what Ernest called an *"unsynchronized passion."*

❦

It may not have been a physical relationship, but they sure knew how to flirt in a letter openly. In one letter dated June 19, 1950, at 4:00 a.m., Ernest had written that Dietrich was so beautiful they needed to make her passport picture 9 foot tall. In this same letter, he asked her

> "What really wanted to do for her life's work. Do you want to break everyone's heart for a mere dime?

He told her that she could break his for a nickel, and he would even bring the nickel."

❦

In another letter, Ernest said to her that every time he held her in his arms, he felt like he was home. At the last of the letter, he said that he loved her and was holding her and kissing her hard.

❦

Ernest wrote to her in 1951 from Cuba where the tropical heat was miserable, and he was trying his best to write "***The Old Man and the Sea***." He told her it was even too hot for making love if she could imagine that unless they were underwater, and he felt he was never good at doing that.

❦

Ernest did reveal to one of his friends as to why he felt their relationship was never consummated. He felt that they were both victims of a passion that was unsynchronized. He said there were times he was out of love, Dietrich was in some deep romantic involvement, and when those occasions when Dietrich was open for a relationship with me, I felt submerged and not open for loving anyone.

❦

In a letter from Dietrich to Ernest, she said that she thought it was the time that she told him that she thought of him all the time. That she read his letters over and over and she did talk about Ernest to a few men she had especially chosen. She confessed she had moved his picture to her bedroom so she could gaze upon it hopelessly.

❧

In the letters, it opens up to their insecurities and their fears and frequently tells of Ernest's fight against depression all his life. In June 1950, he said that wars are nothing but spinach. Life alone was the hard part.

❧

Dietrich never made a secret of how much she disliked physical relationships. For that reason maybe she was not a bad match for Ernest, even with his womanizing reputation.

❧

When Ernest referred to Mary Welsh, his fourth wife, he said that Mary was the best he had ever known in bed. Ernest said he had not been around many women and was shy. Who in the world could believe any of that?

❧

Dietrich lived her last ten years bed-ridden in her house in Paris, and in 1992 she died of renal failure.

❧ VI ❧
ERNEST'S CHALLENGES WITH MENTAL ISSUES

«There is nothing noble in being superior to your fellow men. True nobility lies in being superior to your former self.»

Ernest Hemingway

❧

Ernest no doubt was captivating to anyone he met, he made friends so easy and loved parties; but he had a temper and an even more massive ego that made it difficult for him to keep friends.

❧

He showed off regularly which made him obnoxious to many, and he was accused all the time of exaggerating or faking his so-called adventures, all the accidents and supposed injuries he had been through while traveling the world. What his listeners did not realize, even though he embellished his stories, some of his injuries were serious, and all in all had led to his health being much worse later on in his life. Hearing him brag made it hard for those listening to him brag and they did not sympathize with Ernest as he had caused most of his problems himself.

❦

Even with his "*alpha male*" focus, he had of himself it seemed he did have a romantic but sensitive side, and with all four of his '*tender*' but '*short*' marriages seem to be products of his real passion. On top of all of this, he was a talented cook.

❦

It seemed for Ernest that war became a potent symbol for the entire world, that he viewed it as being very complex, offered unavoidable pain, destruction, hurt, and filled with all types of moral ambiguities.

❦

Ernest felt to be able to survive in this world, and be able to emerge as a victor; one has to conduct themselves with courage, honor, dignity, endurance, along with traditional principles that came to be "*the Hemingway code*."

❦

Ernest had a way of writing that was widely imitated during the 20th century. It seemed to strip away his using the

inessentials of language, getting rid of the traces of embellish-
ment, sentimentality, and verbosity while striving to be as
honest and as objective as possible.

❧

Ernest found a way to describe a group of actions by his use
of simple, short sentences where all emotional and rhetorical
comments were eliminated. He composed these sentences
with mostly verbs and nouns and a few adverbs and adjectives
and relied on rhythm and repetition for their effect. It comes
out as a precise, but concentrated prose is unemotional and
concrete and yet capable of conveying great irony.

❧

It resulted in rich prose that was concise, unemotional and
concrete but was Ernest's way of using dialogue that was
simple, fresh, and sounded natural. It seemed this style influ-
enced the world over wherever any novel was written, especially from 1930 through the 1950s.

❧

It was but a few short months after Martha and Ernest had
moved into their new home in Ketchum, Idaho that Ernest
was admitted to Mayo Clinic for treatment for high blood
pressure and depression or at least that is what the public was
told. (He would later be treated with shock therapy.)

❧

After Ernest published *"**The Old Man and the Sea**"* in 1952,
Ernest went into crippling despair, writer's block, underwent

repeated shock therapy to try and cure his worsening thoughts about committing suicide. The idea of Ernest wanting to commit suicide just did not fit with his heroic image. It just did not make sense.

⚜

Ernest put forth an outward self-confidence that was masking a more profound pain on the inside, and it seemed throughout his life, he would silently suffer dark times of paranoia, depression, and loneliness that he would try to chase away by drinking.

⚜

After Ernest had lived through not one, but two plane crashes in Africa, he started to get worse with depression and anxiety.

⚜

Even with all his ailments, Mary and Ernest went to Venice for one last time and then went back to Cuba. October 28th, 1954 Ernest was awarded the "***Nobel Prize for Literature***," but because of his injuries could not attend the award cere- mony in Sweden. He sent a written acceptance to be read by John Cabot, who served as the US Ambassador for Sweden.

⚜

1954 was over, but for Ernest, he battled, even more, deterio- rating health that usually would not let him even work. When he did work, he did not feel good about his work. He wrote about 200,000 words on his version of his safari that he considered was doomed and temporarily named it "*African Journal*," but was edited heavily in 1999 and published as "*True At First Light*." Ernest struggled, but for a way to satisfy his 'compulsion' to write he decided to return to the subjects, he felt he knew best and was able to write about without struggling.

❧❧❧

Life Magazine in 1959 contracted Ernest to write a short story/article about the bullfights between Louis Miguel Dominguin and Antonio Ordonez who were two of Spain's best matadors.

❧❧❧

Ernest spent the summer of 1959 following the bullfighters to gather material for the article. But, when he started writing this short story/article, it ballooned to 120,000 words. Ernest could not find a way to shorten it. He called upon one of his friends, A. E. Hotchner for helping (something he had never done in his life) to help him cut it down to at least 65,000 words. The magazine had reservations about the length but decided to publish it in three different installments during 1960 under the name of "T*he Dangerous Summer*." It would be the last of his work he would see published during his lifetime.

❧❧❧

Today, there is so much medical information that gives us bizarre malfunctions of our bodies that we would have never dreamed of the effects on the brain, so it is easy to forget in

Ernest's time what a stigma mental illness carried with it; far different than what it is today.

❧

Most do not realize that there might have been much more going on in Ernest mind than anyone ever guessed. In 2006 a psychiatrist reviewing his medical records determined that by the time Ernest died, he probably was suffering from alcohol dependence, bipolar disorder, the probability of borderline narcissistic personality, and from traumatic brain injury. It was also felt that part of all the brain damage issues had been caused by the several concussions he had suffered from (two of which were from the plane crashes that happened in Africa), and his heavy drinking.

❧

The psychiatrist also talked about when Ernest was a child, how his mom would dress him as a girl, how his dad would beat him, how Ernest would hide and aim a loaded gun at his Dad's head.

❧

Some of the doctors were sure that he had no mental illness, but he had a disease that was hereditary in some families that was caused by having too much iron in the blood. It was called hemochromatosis and could be responsible for the problems Ernest and his family suffered.

❧

Suicide ran rampant in Ernest's family like an ugly red line.

Three of Dr. Clarence Hemingway's children – Ursula, Ernest, and Leicester who were the children that had found Clarence's body – committed suicide. Then a granddaughter of Ernest's by the name of Margaux Hemingway committed suicide when she was 41 years old.

⚜

Many who have reviewed his medical records feel his suicide was because his doctors were responsible for malpractice and they had failed to be able to diagnose him with hemochromatosis. It was a hereditary disease that was easily treatable and well enough known about that he should have never had any suffering from the illness during all those years. His doctors missed every sign and symptom that Ernest exhibited; even though he was a textbook case. It was so easy to treat, and they could have been able to prevent all his disabilities.

⚜

Hemochromatosis is found more often in people of Scottish, Irish, Welsh, and the other northern European descents. Ernest was of Celtic heritage. There are about one per each two hundred North Americans that suffer from hemochromatosis, and almost 20% carry the recessive gene that is associated with the disease.

ERNEST'S DOCTORS FAILED HIM
MISERABLY

౿ఌ

When you see a doctor for the first time, they take your family history as it gives them a good idea of problems you might be prone to inherit. Each time you come back to your doctor, they will revisit that history and see if you have developed any symptoms that might now be showing up at your time of life that was not showing up at your last visit that exhibits some of the family symptoms.

All of his other family members who had committed suicide probably had the very same, very treatable disease. His dad had diabetes, memory loss, depression and later in life, his skin turned to bronze. And, Ernest, followed closely in his footsteps.

There was something that was damaging and killing every cell in Ernest's body. He was going to every doctor he could think of for treating his severe heart disease, cirrhosis of his liver, treating his arthritis, hardening of his arteries, depression, diabetes, and losing his teeth. During the most significant part of his life, Ernest would try drinking gin and lime, Angostura bitters, tomato juice, and beer, or absinthe and champagne to try to treat the pain that racked his body.

Whatever it was, it was damaging his brain at the same time. If only his doctors had run a simple blood test, it would have given them the correct diagnosis so they could treat this illness.

HOW HEMOCHROMATOSIS CAN
DIMINISH YOUR BRAIN
AND BODY

You must have iron to live as it aids in carrying oxygen and is necessary for many of the body's chemical reactions. Iron is also a potent oxidant that can dump inside and damage your cells through your entire body if you have too much of it. To you avoid getting iron poisoning, the intestines will stop absorbing the iron when it says you have had enough.

Patients that have hemochromatosis are not able to stop the absorption of iron when they get too much, so the iron keeps accumulating and depositing:
   • in the brain where it can cause memory loss, depression, and cause problems with every brain function
   • cause cirrhosis of the liver
   • cause diabetes by damaging the pancreas
   • in the skin turning it to bronze
   • in the joints causing painful, horrible arthritis
   • in the eyes causing blindness

A SIMPLE TREATMENT FOR
HEMOCHROMATOSIS

If the iron levels of this disease can be kept within the normal range, there will be no tissue damage and the patient can live a normal life. The patient will need to visit with the doctor every few months, have a ferritin blood test that will measure how much iron is being deposited in the patient's tissues. When the ferritin levels get too high, the one or two pints of blood is withdrawn from the patient. The blood itself is usually perfectly healthy and can be given to others, but most blood banks will refuse to use it.

WHAT WOULD HAVE HAPPENED
TO ERNEST IF THEY HAD
DIAGNOSED HIM SOONER?

The gorgeous landscapes of Idaho were not able to hide the fact that there was something wrong with Ernest. During the fall of 1960, Ernest was flown to Rochester, Minnesota to the Mayo Clinic. Outside the family, people were being told that he was being treated for high blood pressure, but in real life, he was there to be treated for depression so severe that Mary, his wife could not handle him anymore. When Ernest started talking about killing himself, his physician at Ketchum said it was time to get expert help.

On arrival at Mayo Ernest was admitted under the name of George Saviers, his doctor back home and they started a medical treatment plan to try to repair him mentally. This treatment plan would eventually lead to shock therapy. The family says that while he was there, he had somewhere between 11-15 shock treatments that in no way benefited him; instead, it seemed to hasten his death.

. . .

Without Ernest's memory, he could not write; he couldn't remember any of the images or facts he needed to recall for creating his books. The writing was now impossible.

The first half of 1961 Ernest fought paranoia and depression; he would see his enemies everywhere he turned and kept threatening suicide every time you turned around.

Ernest's physical deterioration was becoming more evident during his 60th year. In pictures, he looks more like he is eighty years old than sixty. There are times one would see him depressed and then at others, he would be the life of the entire party, his mood swings seemed to be exacerbated with his drinking so heavily by at least a quart of liquor a day, and it was taking a significant toll on all of those who were so close to him.

Ernest was at Mayo for seven weeks before being discharged to home. It seemed he had entered a time of wellness. He was sleeping well, eating well, and was limiting his drinking. He was set on a strict writing regimen and was working hard again on a book about the memoir of his time in Paris while he was a youth in the book, "A Moveable Feast."

Then, Ernest's depression started to return slowly to take back Ernest. He was losing his ability to write; he would break down into tears when he could not think of the words he needed to write.

· · ·

Mary found him in April of 1961 as he was starting to load a shotgun. At this point, they hospitalized him near his home in Ketchum, Idaho. He was not there long when he asked if he could go back home to get a few of his belongings. He was escorted by hospital staff, but he still ran from them, grabbed a shotgun, and turned it on himself. The hospital crew caught him, and there was a struggle in which they disarmed him of the gun.

He was sent back to Mayo Clinic for a second time, but when the plane stopped for fuel in South Dakota, Ernest started walking toward another plane's rotating propeller, only stopping because the pilot cut the engine.

It was the third time Ernest had tried to kill himself in four days. He was hospitalized in Mayo this time for two months with more "shock therapy." He was discharged on June 26th, 1961.

Mary felt that Ernest had charmed his doctor at Mayo into the conclusion that he was sane again. The day after they got home, they decided to go out to eat, and Earnest told Mary that the patrons in the dining area were all FBI agents and were there to monitor him. There was no way he was well.

July 2nd, 1961 Ernest woke up before Mary, got a double barrel shotgun out of the downstairs closet and as Mary slept away upstairs, Ernest loaded the gun; then placed the barrel of it in his mouth and finally finished the act that he had been working to accomplish for so long now. It brought his horrible suffering to what has always been known to the world as a tragic and abrupt end.

HEMINGWAY'S SUICIDE NOTE

J uly 2nd is the 53rd anniversary of an epochal event in American literature: the suicide via shotgun to the mouth of the famous Ernest Hemingway.

His wife Mary and sons Bumpy (Jack), Mousy (Patrick), all claimed that Ernest had left no suicide note. But, it is so inconceivable that the most excellent writer of the 20th century didn't write anything at the end of his life.

After more than half a century, there has been found a suicide note written by Ernest. It is below:

July 2nd, 1961 at 6:14 a.m.

Mary, Bumby, Mousy, Rest of the Gang,

. . .

I have been thinking. Tough after all the electro-shock. But here goes.

What will Hemingway leave behind? A few good books? OK. That ought to be it for the obit. 'He wrote a few good books.'

Yes, there was the drinking and the hunting and the whoring and the fishing. And the talking about the drinking and the hunting and the whoring and the fishing. That was all good too. But that was for pal consumption by invitation only.

Always hated the star part. Shy as a doe under this elephant hide. Only thing hated more than signing name on checks to the tax-man, signing it on dog-eared editions of The Sun Also Rises. Hating fame does not keep it away. Swat a fly, ten more appear.

Do they read even the few good books anymore? Nope. Only people who read The Old Man and the Sea were thirty Swedish nitwits in Stockholm. The Nobel Prize for Nitwiterature.

So What has Hemingway left behind? Well, this...

Every young punk with a Liberal Arts degree and a chinful of fuzz and his huevos bursting with juice wants to be ... Hemingway.

Two generations of them now. At least the one in the '30s had some politics, fought wars, fished fish, whored whores. Knew how to read and shoot and drink and talk. A few even knew the back end of a bull from the front.

But this second one, these crew-cut, corn-fed Eisenhower mommy-boys? Who's never seen a comrade shot dead at their side or an elk breaking cover at first light? With their butts like the fenders of a '55 Chevy, unread paperbacks in the back-pockets of their chinos, babbling bits of Spanish to each other but never to Spaniards, the only hard muscle in their soft bodies that faithful drinking arm...

They think all that is ... being Hemingway.

In Havana, the Gloridita was full of them. Couldn't go in there anymore. Key West the same. '59 encierro in Pamplona, punk comes up in the Txoko Bar, me talking quietly with Antonio after a good fight... Wants me to drink from his damn bota. Threw it in the street. Him after it. Can't go back there either. Won't be able to go anywhere soon. A world full of wanna-be Hemingways.

That is all Hemingway's left behind: a bushy salt-and-pepper beard and an ever-faithful drinking arm.

Time to check out gang. A quick clean kill.

The sun also sets.

But, here's the beauty part. Forty, fifty years from now, when all the wanna-be Hemingways are old and fat, and their chin-fuzz is fried to a bristle, and their heroes have dried up like figs in a dusty street... But they still want to do it all like Hemingway...

They will all have to eat a shotgun too.

Adios.

His note was rambling; he left nothing in it about his love for his children or wife; he did not make a lot of sense throughout the entire note. He did not apologize for any mistakes he had made in life or how he may have hurt others. His spelling and grammar were atrocious as he wrote, but that may have been due to all his mental issues and many brain traumas he had suffered. He felt like everyone in the world wanted to be him, Ernest Hemingway.

In this writer's opinion, it sounded much like the grandiose ideas of someone in a manic phase of bipolar disorder. Considering he also carried the diagnosis of a narcissist he also seemed to exhibit that in the letter as well. Everything was all about Ernest. I feel sure between the Hemochromatosis, the bipolar disorder, and the narcissistic issues that none of it played well when he became so determined to kill himself. I am sure you have heard this common saying that

"Where there is a Will, there is a Way." Well, I guess Ernest was Will, and he had met Way early that morning in the form of a bullet.

�֍ VII ✿

ERNEST'S REAL LOVES –
HIS CATS

«The shortest answer is doing the thing.»

Ernest Hemingway

✿✿✿

I have left the cats in Ernest's life until almost the last part of the story because his love for his pets seems so strange for a man that was such a big game hunter and so legendary for his bullish ways.

✿✿✿

When Ernest would be in the boat docks and the bars located near his home in Key West, Ernest had heard tales of a six-toed cat that had powers of magic. There were captains of ships that brought the six-toed cats on board their ships for safe passages and good luck on their journey. The captains that were less superstitious wanted them along so they could catch rats.

❧

The story is not very clear as to how Captain Stanley Dexter got involved, but he somehow heard Hemingway was interested in his famous six-toed cats he called his feline gypsies. Dexter gifted Ernest with one of the famous six-toed precious felines. Ernest's sons Gregory and Patrick gave the kitten the name of a famous movie and film at that time – Snow White.

❧

From Snow White came all the rest of the entire clan and I mean litter after litter of the gypsy cats. Ernest was rumored to have a total of over 150 cats between his houses in Cuba and Key West.

❧

Ernest Hemingway always appreciated a good story. The legend of the nautical "*gypsy cats*" would be no exception for him.

❧

At this time you will find if you visit Ernest's Home and Museum at Key West on Whitehead Street you would see 56 cats. The six-toed cats all have full run of any room in Ernest's home. Almost half of those cats do have six toes, but every one of them carries the gene for polydactyly which means the "*normal*" toed cats can still bear kittens with six toes.

Ernest was known for naming all his cats for famous people, a tradition that staff carries on today. Ernest's home '*app*' lists every cat by their name, favorite spot where they hang out, and their birthday. If you are trying to find Gertrude Stein, most likely you will see the tortoiseshell cat out on the walkway near the housing where staff lives.

❧

The six-toed cats are adorable, but in reality, it is a deformity, the museum curator will explain to everyone.

❧

Another oddity you might notice is that some of the cats have six toes on one of their paws and sometimes they will have seven. You will be able to find every color of a cat or mixed color you would want from Tabbies to Tuxedo cats. Males, females, small cats, and big cats.

❧

So that Snow White's legacy lives on, the house staff will let one kitten have a litter of babies every year. After that, all the rest of the animals will be either neutered or spayed.

❧

The cats all get regular treatment at the resident from one particular veterinarian. At the first of each month, each cat is given heart-worm and flea treatments. Their vaccines are given annually. All cats have dental and health insurance.

❦

Some of the cats live to age 22 because they receive such great care. The cats at Ernest's house see the vet more often than most cat owners will take their cat to the veterinarian in a lifetime.

❦

The primary caretakers for the cats are the housekeeping staff. They feed the cats almost two TONS of dry cat food every year; with the older cats who have bad teeth, they will be fed soft canned cat food. They are fed every day at 8:00 a.m. and 4:00 p.m. at various water and feeding stations all through the house. On the grounds, there is a cemetery designated for the cats.

❦

Currently, the kitties that are crossing over the rainbow bridge now are being cremated. One of the last cat bodies buried in the pet cemetery was that of Marilyn Monroe. As she was buried, they sang '*Candle in the Wind*.'

❦

There is a sign at the front gate that asks all guest to please not pick up any of the cats. You can pet them, talk to them, or ask them for individual consultation; but please do not pick them up.

People who were never fans of Ernest's books or his story-telling, like to come to this home to see the beautiful architecture, the lush gardens, the history, and some come only to see the multi-toed cats.

Any visitor to the Hemingway home knows that the house has more than Ernest's typewriter, the very used urinal that he had drug home from Sloppy Joe's bar, and the bed that was white iron-framed.

The six-toed cats are considered to be good luck, but their luck has been powerless against federal regulators.

The museum had a nine-year bid to keep all the cats out of reach from the Department of Agriculture, but it ended. The case went to the US Court of Appeals as the 11th Circuit had ruled the agency can regulate all the cats under the reach of the Animal Welfare Act. They can do this because this same act applies to travel circus animals, zoos, because the Hemingway Museum uses the cats in advertisements, sells merchandise for cats to tourists.

To make it short and sweet, his cats are a breathing, living exhibit and because of that, they require a federal license.

❧

The tale of the cats is not more than the federal government running over the little man and their state and local laws that can govern domesticated animals.

❧

At one point the Department of Agriculture sent the group for the Ethical Treatment of Animals to review what the actual situation was in 2005. The final review revealed that all they found was a bunch of happy, relaxed, fat cats.

❧

The appeals court agreed the museum always fed, kept, and they provide veterinary care weekly for all the cats. The three judges were understanding. They went on to say that the museum was in a unique situation and they did sympathize with the museum's position. But, they felt it was not the court's place to be evaluating federal regulations.

❧

The museum settled with the Department of Agriculture in 2008 in that it would grant them to allow things stay as they were IF they heightened the fence, added some unique bowls that had been planned to drown bugs and also upgrade their cat shelters.

ERNEST AND HIS GOOD FRIEND
IVANCICH

❧

There have been fifteen letters revealed in the JFK Presidential Library & Museum that had been written by Ernest to his good friend Ivancich. They had met in a bar in Venice in 1949. They bonded over the leg wounds they had both got during the war. When Ivancich went to Cuba to find work, he stayed with Ernest at his home, the Finca Vigia, and it is felt that when Ernest visited with Ivancich's sister, Adriana, it inspired Hemingway on to his creative side for when he wrote "*The Old Man and the Sea*." The two men wrote and maintained a close friendship until Ernest killed himself in 1961.

❧

It was in February of 1953, Ernest told Ivancich about how badly he felt when he had to kill his cat, Willie, right after it was run over by a car. He said he missed Uncle Willie. Said he had had to shoot people before in war but had never had to kill anyone or anything that he had loved or known for eleven years; or anything that had two broken legs and purred.

Ernest told of a group of tourists that showed up at his house that terrible day, and he was still holding his rifle, and he tried to explain and tell them they were coming during the wrong time and to please understand and leave. The rich guy in the Cadillac said to him that he felt they had arrived at an excellent time to see the great Ernest crying because he had to kill one of his cats. People, in general, can be so heartless.

Ernest told Ivancich that he wished he could write letters as good as he did. He said he felt that since he wrote all day long that at the end of the day he felt all written out.

Ernest was said to have always taken great pleasure when he wrote about his family and his cats. Both of them seemed to play an essential role in his life. They both played a part that would show his softer side other than his usual macho man of the fisherman and hunter.

His cats he called "*love sponges*" and "*purr factories*."

It seems you can't write about Ernest and talk about his family life, the women he claimed he loved, the fact he was a man whore and his cats. His last cat was named Big Boy Peterson. He and first wife, Hadley had a cat named Feather Cat when they lived in Toronto, and a cat named F. Puss in Paris who Ernest said was a great babysitter for their first-born son.

❧

Third wife, Martha convinced him to buy Finca Vigia, a farm in Cuba that had several buildings and multiple stray cats. Ernest brought in more cats there on the farm; Persian Princessa, Willie and Dillinger, and Angora Good Will. They mated Boise and Princessa, and after that, many litters followed.

❧

There were not just cats, but dogs found their way into Ernest home as well. It started with Wax Puppy that he had brought home for Hadley when they lived in Paris. While in Cuba he took in a bunch of small mixed-breed dogs that had curled tails. There was one, in particular, Negrita that just stole his heart. On one of their trips to Idaho, they picked up Black Dog who was a Springer Spaniel that they took back to Cuba with them to join the rest of their animal clan.

❧

At one point in Ernest's life, he was living in a cave some-where in Paris as a young man, and he said that he was so poor he couldn't even afford a cat. Hemingway had gentle manners and a low voice, so he was more like a cat and dog whisperer. He felt that each one of his pets were individuals, each having their personality, and he professed that cats had an absolute emotional honesty.

VIII
WHERE ERNEST FINALLY GOT TO REST

«Man is not made for defeat.»

Ernest Hemingway

To go over his immediate family: Ernest was married at least four different times: 1921-1927 Hadley Richardson, 1927-1940 Pauline Pfeiffer, 1940-1945 Martha Gellhorn, and in 1946 Mary Welsh. He was the father to three boys: with Hadley in 1923 was born John Hadley Nicanor who they nicknamed "***Bumby***," Patrick was given birth by Pauline in 1928; as well as Gregory in 1931 by Pauline.

He wrote one novel, "***Across the River and into the Trees***" (1950), about an army officer that died while he was on leave in the city of Venice. For this novel, he won the Nobel Prize in Literature in 1954.

❧

After his death and the finding of several manuscripts three more novels emerged and were published: "*Islands in the Stream*" 1970; "*The Garden of Eden*" 1986; and "*True at First Light*" 1999 and the same for his memoir "A Moveable Feast" 1964.

❧

Ernest's intense approach to life, his fantastic work made him the most influential writer in America during the twentieth century.

❧

Ernest's legacy was that of a loud man who drank too much all the time, being a very masculine man, loving lots of women, telling false stories, and bragging all the time, traveling the world it seems funny to see where he is buried. Where the grave lies in the small Ketchum, Idaho cemetery of this famous man, you will find nothing but an unadorned, flat slab which looks like concrete but is probably granite that is worn away. The slab lays flat on the ground and is a long rectangle that only has his name and the date of birth and death listed on it. No matter what it seems like it has not stopped any of his fans from leaving their sympathies with flowers, booze, and coins to this day.

❧

Ernest Hemingway was only 29 when his father committed suicide Ernest always predicted that he would probably die the same way. It seems that Ernest Hemingway knew precisely what he was talking about and this time he was not bragging or boasting.

❧ IX ❧

CONCLUSION

❀❀❀

Ernest Miller Hemingway was born with a silver spoon in his mouth one could say, and his parents were able to expose him and his siblings to different adventures, mostly those around Lake Michigan in the summer months.

❀❀❀

He knew as early as in his High School years that he wanted to write for a living. It was what made him breathe. Starting out writing for newspapers, then as a war correspondent and on to writing books that became favorite best sellers made him known as a famous author quickly.

❀❀❀

He never went at the work of being a writer to become

famous, but it did not matter as he loved to write and his method of writing was trying to be imitated by many other writers, but no one could seem ever to pick up his ability to write and pull people into his stories like Ernest could.

Ernest lived life large until the last four or five years when his mental health started declining rapidly. He had abused his body so much during his younger adult years that it too was speeding him along to fatality even quicker with his mental decline.

Reaching his goal of suicide was thwarted so many times that he must have almost felt relief when he finally accomplished the task he had set before himself for so long.

STRENGTHS & WEAKNESSES

STRENGTHS

- Seemed not to be afraid of whatever trial he was about to face. When caught in a bad or dangerous situation he never gave up but kept on going until he found a way out. Like he never ran out of adrenaline.
- Women swooned over him. All he had to do was to look their way, and they seemed to be putty in his hands.
- He was an extremely talented writer in the 19th and 20th century rivaled by none.
- He made friends all over the world; and was a wealth of information.
- He loved animals, especially cats and some dogs.
- He enjoyed to the highest degree fishing and hunting.

WEAKNESSES

- He was a braggart and a boaster who had grandiose ideas of himself; that made a lot of people sick to be around him.
- Mentally, he became weak at a young age; no one realized it.
- He made rash decisions that came back to bite him later in life.
- He was a womanizer, and it seemed he had to change wives every 5-6 years. When he got tired of one, he had another picked out to take the place of the one he was about to divorce.
- When he was married, he would still cheat on his current wife with other women even if it was only in lustful, heated, romantic letters.
- He seemed to care only for himself most of the time; even though all references state that he cared for his family. It is hard to believe that he did care for his family since he changed wives so often and cheated on his current wives constantly. He hated both of his parents; he never seemed to care for his siblings as he never spoke of them. For his children, he never talked much about them, and he was gone from home 75% of the time rather than at home with his family. He was the one that wanted all the luxury and the thrills of life.
- His genetics were against him from day one, and the physicians were all idiots during his time to not identify what caused his entire family to keep committing suicide. Ernest was walking at the edge of the cliff for years waiting for that final push.

❧ X ❧
THREE MORE INFORMATIVE BOOKS ON ERNEST MILLER HEMINGWAY

❦

- The Letters of Ernest Hemingway: 3 Volume Set. Cambridge Edition of his letters by Ernest Hemingway
- Ernest Hemingway: A Life from Beginning to End by Hourly History
- American Legends: The Life of Ernest Hemingway by Charles River Editors

YOUR FREE EBOOK!

As a way of saying thank you for reading our book, we're offering you a free copy of the below eBook.

Happy Reading!

Made in the USA
Columbia, SC
30 September 2020